IN THE NEWS Need to Know

NATO

by Ashley Kuehl

Consultant: Caitlin Krieck, Social Studies Teacher and Instructional Coach, The Lab School of Washington

Minneapolis, Minnesota

Credits

Cover and title page, © Public Domain/Wikimedia; 5, © KENZO TRIBOUILLARD/Getty Images; 7, © Alexandros Michailidis/Shutterstock; 9, © Sean Gallup/Getty Images; 11, © Peteri/Shutterstock; 12, © Public Domain/Wikimedia; 13, © Popperfoto/Getty Images; 15T, © AFP/Getty Images; 15B, © Musomo/Shutterstock; 17, © Keystone-France/Getty Images; 19, © Liu Heung Shing/AP Images; 21, © ROBERT VANDEN BRUGGE/Getty Images; 23, © Ezra Shaw/Getty Images; 25, © Anadolu/Getty Images; 27, © Bloomberg/Getty Images; 28TL, © Public Domain/Wikimedia; 28ML, © Bloomberg/Getty Images; 28BL, © Frederic GARRIDO-RAMIREZ/NATO

Bearport Publishing Company Product Development Team

Publisher: Jen Jenson; Director of Product Development: Spencer Brinker; Managing Editor: Allison Juda; Editor: Cole Nelson; Associate Editor: Naomi Reich; Associate Editor: Tiana Tran; Art Director: Colin O'Dea; Designer: Kim Jones; Designer: Kayla Eggert; Product Development Specialist: Owen Hamlin

Statement on Usage of Generative Artificial Intelligence

Bearport Publishing remains committed to publishing high-quality nonfiction books. Therefore, we restrict the use of generative AI to ensure accuracy of all text and visual components pertaining to a book's subject. See BearportPublishing.com for details.

Quote Sources

Page 28: Joe Biden from "Statement from President Joe Biden Welcoming Sweden to NATO," *Whitehouse.gov*, March 7, 2024; Jens Stoltenberg from "Speech by NATO Secretary General Jens Stoltenberg on the occasion of NATO's 75th anniversary celebration with the Chair of the NATO Military Committee and Ministers of Foreign Affairs," *nato.int*, April 4, 2024; Farah Dakhlallah, from "Meet Farah Dakhlallah, NATO's First Spokesperson of Arab Descent," *Al-Monitor*, February 28, 2024.

Library of Congress Cataloging-in-Publication Data is available at www.loc.gov or upon request from the publisher.

ISBN: 979-8-89232-764-0 (hardcover)
ISBN: 979-8-89232-942-2 (paperback)
ISBN: 979-8-89232-851-7 (ebook)

For more information, write to Bearport Publishing, 5357 Penn Avenue South, Minneapolis, MN 55419.

Contents

From Neutral to NATO

In March 2024, Sweden joined the North Atlantic **Treaty** Organization (NATO). Sweden's flag went up next to 31 others. Sweden was now an **ally** to these countries. They agreed to help keep peace around the world. If needed, they would also follow these allies into war.

Sweden was neutral for more than 200 years. They did not take sides during wars. Joining NATO means Sweden promises to **protect** NATO allies.

Sweden's blue-and-yellow flag flies outside NATO headquarters.

A Treaty to Protect

NATO gets its name from where its countries are found. Most members are in the north. Almost all NATO countries are near the Atlantic Ocean.

Each of these countries signed a treaty. This written agreement says NATO will protect peace and democracy around the world.

NATO countries give money to help the group. Some members have more money to send. Smaller countries with less money are asked to give less.

NATO headquarters has been in Brussels, Belgium, since 1967.

Working as a group makes NATO stronger. The group has more **resources** together.

Working together also keeps everyone safer. Other countries do not want to fight all of NATO. This may stop these countries from attacking a member of NATO.

NATO does not have its own military. NATO countries send troops when they are needed. The soldiers work together.

After the War

NATO started after World War II (1939–1945). The war hurt many countries in Europe. Bombs destroyed their buildings. Many people died. At the same time, the Soviet Union was getting stronger. It wanted to take over more land.

The Soviet Union was made up of 15 countries. It included the countries that are now Russia, Ukraine, and Belarus.

The Soviet Union in 1949

The Soviet Union made other countries worried. Many European countries could not fight back if the Soviet Union attacked.

So, they came together. Canada and the United States joined 10 European countries to protect one another.

The United States dropped two **atomic bombs** at the end of World War II. This killed more than 100,000 people. The Soviet Union made their own atomic bombs soon after.

Twelve as One

Leaders from these first 12 countries met in Washington, D.C. in 1949. They wrote the **terms** of the treaty. Signing gave each country protection.

But if another NATO country was attacked, each ally had to go to war, too. This made signing the treaty risky.

More countries were added to NATO over time. Turkey and Greece joined in 1952. West Germany joined three years later. Spain was added in 1982.

The signing ceremony of the North Atlantic Treaty
MEMBERS 1949
JOINED 1950–1996
JOINED 1997–2022
JOINED 2023
JOINED 2024
North America
Atlantic Ocean
Europe

NATO and the Warsaw Pact

The Soviet Union formed its own agreement in 1955. It joined with seven allies to make an agreement called the Warsaw **Pact**.

These countries protected one another just like NATO. But the Soviet Union also used the pact to control its allies.

Many countries in Eastern Europe joined the Warsaw Pact. This included Albania, Romania, and Hungary. Bulgaria, Poland, East Germany, and Czechoslovakia also joined.

Signing of the Warsaw Pact

The power of the Warsaw Pact and NATO stopped the United States and the Soviet Union from fighting each other. However, there was **tension** between both sides. Both countries and their allies spied on one another.

Over time, the Soviet Union slowly lost power. Countries started leaving the Warsaw Pact. By 1991, the Soviet Union broke apart. The pact ended.

This time of tension was called the **Cold War** (1947–1991). The United States and the Soviet Union entered other fights. The two countries helped different sides during wars in Korea and Vietnam.

The last leader of the Soviet Union, Mikhail Gorbachev

Partners or Members?

When the Warsaw Pact ended, some of its countries asked to join NATO. At first, they were not allowed to be members. NATO agreed to help them as partners. But Hungary, Poland, and the Czech Republic still wanted to join the treaty. In 1999, they finally became full members.

For a new country to join NATO, current members must all agree. This can take years. Any NATO member can block a country from joining.

NATO leaders welcomed partner countries as full members in 1999.

A Promise to Defend

NATO did not need to go to war for many years. This changed on September 11, 2001. **Terrorists** flew planes into buildings in New York City and Washington, D.C. A third plane crashed in Pennsylvania. Nearly 3,000 people died. NATO joined together to defend the United States.

In 2001, NATO allies went to Afghanistan. They fought the group that had attacked the United States. NATO soldiers left the country in 2021.

NYC
fashion

How NATO Works

Going to war in 2001 was a big decision. How does the organization choose what to do? NATO holds **summits**. These are big meetings. They are where the organization talks about going to war.

Summits are also where NATO adds more countries. NATO has added more than a dozen members since 2004.

The North Atlantic Council makes NATO's day-to-day decisions. It has people from all NATO countries.

NATO summits take place at the NATO headquarters.

Today and Tomorrow

As times change, NATO will need to keep up. Other countries want to join NATO. But more members would mean more countries to protect.

NATO is also facing new kinds of threats. It is working on ways to fight **cyberattacks**. It also plans to help with disasters caused by climate change.

Ukraine has wanted to join NATO since 2008. But the country has had conflicts with Russia. Some NATO members worry what this would mean for the organization.

NATO security experts train to stop cyberattacks.

Voices in the News

People have many things to say about NATO. Some of their voices can be heard in the news.

Joe Biden
Former United States president

"NATO will continue to stand for freedom and democracy for generations to come."

Jens Stoltenberg
Former NATO secretary general

"Today, NATO is bigger, stronger, and more united than ever."

Farah Dakhlallah
NATO spokesperson

"NATO protects more than one billion people, safeguarding their freedom and democracy and contributing to a more peaceful world."

SilverTips for SUCCESS

★SilverTips for REVIEW

Review what you've learned. Use the text to help you.

Define key terms

allies
defend
summit
treaty
Warsaw Pact

Check for understanding

What does NATO stand for? And where does the name come from?

Why did NATO start?

What do the member countries do for one another and the rest of the world?

Think deeper

Do you think NATO makes its member countries safer? Why or why not?

★SilverTips on TEST-TAKING

- **Make a study plan.** Ask your teacher what the test is going to cover. Then, set aside time to study a little bit every day.
- **Read all the questions carefully.** Be sure you know what is being asked.
- **Skip any questions** you don't know how to answer right away. Mark them and come back later if you have time.

Glossary

ally a nation that works with others toward a common cause

atomic bombs very powerful bombs that can destroy entire cities

cold war a struggle between two nations that does not include physical fighting

cyberattacks attempts to break into computers illegally to cause damage or harm

protect to keep safe from harm

resource something useful or valuable

summits meetings between powerful leaders

tension a state of unfriendliness between individuals or groups

terms conditions of an agreement

terrorists people or groups that use violence or threats to gain power

treaty an agreement between countries or other political groups

Read More

Faust, Daniel R. *The Cold War (World History: Need to Know).* Minneapolis: Bearport Publishing, 2024.

Gieseke, Tyler. *NATO (Crisis in Ukraine).* Minneapolis: Abdo, 2023.

Moening, Kate. *The Cold War (War Histories).* Minneapolis: Bellwether Media, 2024.

Learn More Online

1. Go to **FactSurfer.com** or scan the QR code below.
2. Enter "**NATO**" into the search box.
3. Click on the cover of this book to see a list of websites.

Index

About the Author

Ashley Kuehl is an editor and writer specializing in nonfiction for young people. She lives in Minneapolis, MN.